MANTLES PAST AND PRESENT OFFICIAL WORKBOOK

WHAT MANTLES ARE AND HOW THEY WORK

ROBERTS LIARDON

Harrison House

Harrison House P.O. Box 310, Shippensburg, PA 17257-0310

This book and all other Harrison House's books are available at Christian bookstores and distributors worldwide.

For Worldwide Distribution.

Reach us on the Internet: www.harrisonhouse.com.

ISBN 13 TP: 9781667508740

ISBN 13 eBook: 9781667508757

CONTENTS

INTRODUCTION

Welcome to the Mantles Past and Present Official Workbook, a guide designed to deepen your understanding of spiritual mantles, their biblical foundations, and their relevance in today's world. This workbook is an invitation to embark on a journey of discovery, where you will explore the intricacies of spiritual inheritances and the roles they play in the lives of believers across generations.

As you open the pages of this workbook, prepare to engage with a rich tapestry of teachings and insights that reveal the dynamics of spiritual mantles. From the mantle of Elijah passed to Elisha to the all-encompassing mantle of Christ given to every believer, this workbook aims to bridge the gap between ancient scriptural mandates and the contemporary callings of the Church.

KEY TAKEAWAYS AND EXPECTATIONS:

- **Understanding of Spiritual Mantles:** Dive into the historical and biblical significance of mantles. You will learn about the different types of mantles mentioned in the Bible, their purposes, and the contexts in which they were used. This foundation will help you recognize and respect the divine empowerments bestowed upon individuals by God throughout history.

- **Relevance of Mantles Today:** Discover how ancient mantles translate into today's spiritual callings. The workbook outlines how modern-day believers can identify and operate under the mantles specific to their callings, whether in ministry, business, or social leadership. You will explore how these mantles are not relics of the past but active and essential elements of God's ongoing plan.

- **Personal Reflection and Application:** Each chapter is structured to not only provide information but also to encourage personal reflection and application. Reflective questions and journaling prompts will guide you to consider how the concepts discussed may be relevant in your own life and ministry. These elements are designed to prompt introspection and personal revelation, fostering a deeper personal relationship with God.

- **Practical Engagement with the Spiritual Realm:** Learn practical ways to engage with the spiritual realm in respect to receiving, recognizing, and walking in a spiritual mantle. This includes teachings on the prerequisites for carrying a mantle, such as holiness, obedience, and divine calling, as well as the responsibilities that come with such spiritual assignments.

- **Preparation for Succession:** The workbook addresses the critical aspect of mantle succession—the passing of spiritual authority from one generation to another. You will gain insights on how to prepare yourself or others to receive a mantle, the importance of divine timing, and the role of mentorship and discipleship in this process.
- **Community and Corporate Mantles:** Explore the concept of corporate mantles, where a specific spiritual empowerment is given to a group or a church community. Discussions will include how these mantles influence collective missions and how they differ from individual mantles in scope and impact.

WHAT YOU CAN EXPECT TO RECEIVE:

- **Deepened Spiritual Insight:** Through the comprehensive study of scriptural examples and contemporary applications, gain a richer understanding of how God uses spiritual mantles to fulfill His purposes on Earth.
- **Enhanced Personal Growth:** Engage with exercises designed to help you identify and cultivate the spiritual gifts and callings that align with potential mantles in your life.
- **Empowered Community Interaction:** Learn how to support and enhance the functioning of spiritual

mantles within your community, contributing to a stronger, more unified body of Christ.

- **Guided Spiritual Practice:** Practical advice on maintaining the integrity of a spiritual mantle and navigating the challenges associated with these divine gifts ensures that you are not just a recipient of knowledge but also a practitioner of spiritual disciplines.

This workbook is not just a collection of teachings; it is a transformative tool designed to equip and inspire. As you proceed, approach each lesson with an open heart and a willing spirit, ready to receive and act upon the revelations God has prepared for you through the study of His Word and His works. Let's begin this journey together, exploring the depths of **Mantles Past and Present** and stepping into the roles God has ordained for us in His grand design.

～

CHAPTER 1
A DIVINE SETUP

Stay open and obedient to God's leading, even when it takes you on unexpected paths. His plans are often hidden in simple daily choices that can lead to profound life-changing encounters.

"Trust in the Lord with all your heart, and lean not on your own understanding; In all your ways acknowledge Him, and He shall direct your paths." - Proverbs 3:5-6 (NKJV)

In the vibrant streets of London in 1962, my decision to take a detour after Bible school led me to what I now understand was a **Divine Appointments**. As I walked through a neighborhood, the engraved name 'George Jeffreys' on a doorplate caught my eye. This wasn't just any name; it was the name of a man whose powerful ministry I had recently studied. I learned that day how God orchestrates our steps, leading us to significant encounters that align with His greater plan.

The importance of knowing and honoring those who have paved the way for us in faith became evident to me as I stood in front of that nameplate. **Heritage of Faith** isn't just about appreciating history—it's about building on the spiritual foundations laid by those before us. George Jeffreys was not just a historical figure; he was a conduit of God's power, having founded the Elim denomination and over 100 churches. His life's work taught me that our actions today can build a legacy that will inspire and equip future generations.

This encounter underscored the **The Power of Legacy**. Witnessing the enduring impact of Jeffreys' ministry reminded me that our spiritual endeavors can ripple through time, affecting lives long after we are gone. It's a powerful reminder that what we do in obedience to God isn't just for our own time but seeds into the future of God's kingdom.

During my visit, I learned more about a particular miracle—a man miraculously healed under Jeffreys' ministry. This man had lived with only one foot but was told to buy a pair of shoes because by morning he would have two feet. Miraculously, it came to pass just as Jeffreys had said. This story is a vivid illustration of the **The Role of Faith in Miracles**. It taught me that our actions, when aligned with God's commands, can lead to the extraordinary, breaking the limits of what we perceive as possible.

That day, when Jeffreys laid his hands on me and prayed, I felt a tangible transfer of spiritual energy and purpose. It was as if the mantle he carried was being passed on to me. This **Spiritual Mantles** moment was not just symbolic but a real impartation of anointing, equipping me to carry forward the healing and evangelistic work that Jeffreys had championed.

The entire experience was a lesson in **Immediate Obedience**. As I acted on the impulse to explore that nameplate further, it led to a life-altering encounter. This taught me that God's nudges, however small they may seem, are often precursors to significant spiritual events. Responding quickly and obediently can open doors to blessings and roles that God has prepared for us.

Witnessing firsthand the effects of a miraculous healing broadened my understanding of **Witnessing God's Glory**. The healed man walking through his village on two feet became a living testimony of God's power. Such testimonies are not just for the one healed but serve as beacons that draw others to God, multiplying the effects of a single act of faith.

The seemingly coincidental meeting with Jeffreys felt orchestrated by a higher plan, a **Prophetic Fulfillment** that seemed aligned perfectly with what I needed at that moment in my spiritual journey. It was a reminder that God is intimately involved in the details of our lives, orchestrating events that fulfill His divine will.

The news of George Jeffreys' passing the day after our meeting marked a poignant **Transition of Spiritual Authority**. It felt as though the spiritual authority he wielded was being handed over to a new generation. This transition was not just about the continuation of ministry but a significant shift in the spiritual landscape, where old mantles find new shoulders to rest upon.

Lastly, this whole experience taught me about **The Impact of Spiritual Preparation**. My years at Bible school had not just been about gaining knowledge but were preparing me spiritually to receive and carry forward the legacy of giants like Jeffreys. Every prayer, every study session, every act of service was part of the divine preparation, equipping me for the moment when the mantle would pass to me.

REFLECTIVE QUESTIONS

1. **Have you experienced a moment that you would consider a divine appointment?** Looking back, I see how these moments have shaped not just my ministry, but also my personal faith journey.

2. **What legacy of faith have you inherited from those who have influenced your spiritual journey?** I've been fortunate to stand on the shoulders of giants—men and women who paved the way with their faithfulness.

3. **In what areas of your life do you need to exercise more immediate obedience to God's instructions?** I've learned that our greatest breakthroughs often follow our immediate response to God's nudges.

4. **How can you better prepare yourself to receive and carry spiritual mantles?** For me, preparation involved not only study and prayer but also seeking out and heeding the wisdom of those who walked the path before me.

5. **Can you identify a time when a simple act of faith led to a significant outcome in your life?** Each act of faith, no matter how small, has woven a larger story of God's faithfulness in my life.

ACTIONABLE STEPS

- **Cultivate a Heart for Obedience:** Each morning, I ask God to help me recognize and respond to His guidance swiftly and faithfully.

- **Equip Yourself with Knowledge of God's Word**: Dedicating time to learn about the lives of those in Scripture who experienced God's divine setup has deepened my understanding of His ways.
- **Engage in Prayer for Divine Appointments**: I make it a point to pray for God to lead me into strategic encounters that fulfill His divine purposes, trusting that He is always at work.

JOURNALING **Prompt**

Reflect on a time when you felt led by God to take an unexpected path. What was the outcome, and how did it deepen your trust in His guidance?

∾

CHAPTER 2
WHAT IS A MANTLE?

Embrace the understanding that God's plans are often much larger than our individual roles. Recognizing and supporting the flow of spiritual mantles can connect us more deeply to His grand design.

"For I know the plans I have for you, declares the Lord, plans for welfare and not for evil, to give you a future and a hope."
- Jeremiah 29:11 (NKJV)

In my journey of understanding and experiencing spiritual truths, I have come to learn about the **Nature of a Mantle**. A mantle is not just a metaphorical garment but a supernatural "cloak" placed by God on chosen individuals. These are the people destined to carry out significant and divine tasks, marking a profound responsibility passed down through generations. This mantle, residing in the realm of the Spirit, signifies a lifetime assignment crucial for executing God's over-arching plan. The continuity and generational aspect of mantles reveal that God's plans are meticulously woven through the ages, touching lives and shaping destinies beyond the immediate.

Exploring further, we find that the term mantle has both **Literal and Figurative Meanings**. Literally, it can be a cloak or shawl, providing physical warmth and protection. Figuratively, it expands to embody significant roles, responsibilities, or anointings passed from one individual to another. This duality helps us grasp the mantle's tangible and intangible aspects, enhancing our understanding of its spiritual weight.

One of the most poignant scriptural examples that illustrate this is the transfer between **Elijah and Elisha**. This event wasn't merely about passing a piece of clothing but symbolized the profound transfer of prophetic authority and responsibilities. Such biblical narratives not only illuminate the **Transfer and Expansion** of spiritual roles but also the deep relational dynamics involved in mentoring and spiritual succession.

The **Spiritual Composition of a Mantle** is fascinating. It's like a fabric woven from various divine threads—each representing different spiritual dimensions such as gifts, anointings, and divine mandates. These threads are not random but are intricately selected and woven by God Himself to equip the mantle-bearer for their divine tasks. Understanding this helps us appreciate the complexity and divine craftsmanship behind each mantle, tailored uniquely for its bearer and their mission.

It's important to recognize that a mantle's impact is not static but dynamic, often undergoing **Multiple Bearers of a Mantle** when a single individual cannot shoulder its entire scope. This is not a division of the mantle's power but a strategic distribution that allows for the fullness of God's plans to unfold through different individuals, each carrying a part of the divine mandate according to their calling and capacity.

Reflecting on complex ministries, such as that of George Jeffreys, helps us appreciate that there can be **Different Aspects,**

One Mantle. His multifaceted mantle included healing evangelism and church planting—areas that require diverse giftings and capacities. This understanding clarifies that while the mantle is one, its manifestations can be diverse, tailored to the missions God sets before each bearer.

Occasionally, the mantle does not pass to an individual but to a group—a **Corporate Reception of a Mantle**. This phenomenon can occur when the scope of the mantle is so vast that it necessitates a collective effort to carry forward the divine agenda, as seen in some church movements and denominational foundations.

The enduring influence of a mantle through generations underscores its **Long-lasting Impact**. As each new bearer steps into their role, they build upon the foundation laid by their predecessors, ensuring that the mantle not only maintains its original intent but also grows in depth and breadth.

In this journey, it is vital for us, the broader Christian community, to develop an acute awareness to **Recognition and Response to a Mantle**. By recognizing when and how mantles operate among us, we can better support and facilitate the divine transactions taking place, ensuring that these heavenly assignments are carried out effectively.

As I write this, I invite you to ponder the roles and responsibilities that you might be carrying. Whether or not they are mantles in the traditional sense, they are significant to the Lord. Each task we undertake, supported by prayer and guided by the Holy Spirit, links us to the divine narrative that God is unfolding in our lives and through our generations. Let us walk this path with reverence, humility, and expectation, always ready to step into or support the passing of a mantle.

REFLECTIVE QUESTIONS

1. **Have you ever felt a specific calling or burden that seems larger than your personal capacity?** Reflect on how this might be a part of a larger mantle you are sharing or carrying.

2. **How do you perceive the continuity of spiritual roles and anointings in your community or church?** Consider how you can support those who might be mantle-bearers.

3. **What can you do to prepare yourself spiritually to either receive or support the transfer of a mantle?** Think about spiritual disciplines that might be helpful.

4. **In what ways can you contribute to a collective effort that might be under a corporate mantle?** Identify areas in your community or ministry where you can offer your talents and time.

5. **How does the concept of a mantle challenge or inspire your understanding of spiritual leadership and legacy?** Reflect on the implications for your own life and ministry.

ACTIONABLE STEPS

- **Cultivate Sensitivity to Spiritual Callings**: Engage in regular prayer and meditation to develop a heightened awareness of God's calling and the possible presence of a mantle in your life.
- **Equip Yourself with Biblical Knowledge**: Study the lives of biblical figures who received and transferred

mantles, such as Elijah and Elisha, to gain insights into how God prepares and uses individuals in significant roles.

- **Engage in Supporting Mantle-Bearers:** Actively look for ways to support and encourage those in your community who you believe are carrying a mantle. This can involve prayer, practical assistance, or simply affirming their calling.

JOURNALING **Prompt**

Reflect on any moments in your life when you felt part of a larger plan or calling that transcended your individual efforts. How did it shape your perspective on working within the Body of Christ?

∾

CHAPTER 3
UNTANGLING THE THREADS

Embrace the pursuit of knowledge and clarity in your spiritual journey. God honors the desire to understand and apply His word accurately in our lives.

"If any of you lacks wisdom, let him ask of God, who gives to all liberally and without reproach, and it will be given to him." - James 1:5 (NKJV)

In the spiritual journey of many believers, especially those in Pentecostal and Charismatic circles, there seems to be a **Confusion in Terminology**. Terms such as "mantles," "anointings," "impartations," and "giftings" are often tossed around, sometimes interchangeably, without a solid grasp of their distinct meanings. This lack of understanding can lead to misconceptions and misapplications in our spiritual practices. It is crucial for us as followers of Christ to distinguish between these terms to ensure that our spiritual discourse and practice are both theologically sound and biblically anchored.

One of the most commonly misused terms in our spiritual

vocabulary is "mantle." Often, we hear people claim they have received or inherited a specific mantle, like that of Kathryn Kuhlman or another well-known spiritual leader. However, the **Misuse of 'Mantle'** is widespread as many fail to grasp that a mantle is not just an anointing or a gift but a specific, lifelong divine assignment given by God to an individual. This mantle is meant for carrying out significant tasks within God's kingdom and is often passed down from one generation to another, requiring a high level of spiritual commitment and maturity.

As we delve deeper, it is essential to clarify what exactly an **Understanding Impartations** and **Anointing Defined** are. An impartation generally refers to the transmission of spiritual gifts or anointings through prayer or the laying on of hands, which empowers another person temporarily or for a specific task. On the other hand, an anointing is a more enduring empowerment by the Holy Spirit to perform tasks that God has set out for an individual, often linked to their specific calling in the body of Christ.

The **Distinction Between Terms** is vital for precise communication and understanding in our spiritual journeys. By understanding each term's unique role and function, we can better navigate our spiritual experiences and the language we use to describe them. This clarity helps in fostering a more profound and accurate engagement with our spiritual practices and discussions.

However, the lack of precision in using these terms can often lead to the **Risks of Misinterpretation**. When believers claim mantles or anointings without true spiritual backing or understanding, it can lead to disillusionment or the mistaken belief that they are spiritually empowered in ways they are not. This not only impacts the individual believer's spiritual growth but can also affect the wider community's perception of spiritual gifts and callings.

Therefore, there is a **Need for Accurate Teaching** on these matters. By providing clear, biblically grounded explanations of what mantles, anointings, and impartations are, we can help prevent the common pitfalls of spiritual misidentification and ensure that the Body of Christ is more effectively equipped for the tasks God has assigned to us.

In scripture, we find **Biblical Examples** such as the transition of Elijah's mantle to Elisha, which illustrate the profound and serious nature of such a spiritual transaction. These examples provide us with concrete models of how God intends for these spiritual tools and responsibilities to be understood and handled.

This brings us to the personal aspect of these spiritual realities—the **Personal Responsibility** every believer has to seek understanding and clarity regarding spiritual terms and their applications. This responsibility extends to how we teach, learn, and talk about spiritual realities within our communities.

Ultimately, this chapter aims to inspire believers to **Encouragement to Seek Understanding**. By embracing the pursuit of deeper knowledge and discernment in the spiritual aspects of our faith, we not only enrich our own spiritual lives but also contribute to the health and maturity of the entire Body of Christ.

This exploration into the nuanced world of spiritual terms is not just academic; it is a journey toward deeper spiritual efficacy and faithfulness. As we untangle these threads together, let us move forward with a commitment to truth, clarity, and the powerful simplicity of the gospel, which guides and shapes all our spiritual experiences.

1. **Have you ever used spiritual terms like "mantle" or "anointing" without fully understanding what they mean?** Reflect on how this might have influenced your spiritual expectations or conversations.
2. **Why is it important to have a clear understanding of terms like mantle, anointing, and impartation in your spiritual life?** Consider how clarity in these areas could impact your approach to ministry and personal growth.
3. **What steps can you take to improve your understanding of these key spiritual concepts?** Identify resources or practices that could help deepen your knowledge.
4. **Can you think of a time when a misunderstanding of these terms led to confusion or conflict within your church or community?** Reflect on how better clarity might have changed the situation.
5. **How does understanding the difference between anointing and impartation affect your view of spiritual experiences?** Explore how this distinction might influence your expectations for spiritual growth and ministry.

ACTIONABLE STEPS

- **Cultivate a Study Habit:** Commit to regular study sessions focused on biblical teachings about spiritual gifts, mantles, and anointings. Use reliable theological resources to build a solid foundation of understanding.

- **Equip Yourself with Knowledge**: Attend workshops, seminars, or classes taught by credible teachers within your church or community who can provide clear explanations and teachings on these concepts.
- **Engage in Community Discussions**: Initiate or participate in discussions within your church or spiritual study groups to explore and clarify these terms. Sharing insights and asking questions can enhance collective understanding.

JOURNALING **Prompt**

Reflect on your current understanding of spiritual terms like mantles, anointings, and impartations. How can you take active steps to align your understanding and usage of these terms with biblical teachings? What resources or practices will you seek out to aid in this pursuit?

∾

CHAPTER 4

THE OPERATION OF MANTLES IN THE NEW TESTAMENT

Let us be diligent in applying the teachings of the New Testament to our understanding of spiritual mantles. As we embrace the Cross, we transform our old selves and clothe ourselves in Christ, stepping into the mantle He has prepared for each of us.

"For as many of you as were baptized into Christ have put on Christ." - Galatians 3:27 (NKJV)

In our journey through the Scriptures and our faith, we come to understand the **Transition Through the Cross**, where every Old Testament concept, including the notion of mantles, is transformed by the sacrifice of Jesus. This transformation ensures that our interpretation and application of spiritual principles are aligned with the new covenant brought forth in the New Testament. A vital realization for every believer is that upon accepting Christ, we are immediately **Clothed with Christ**. This is the most significant mantle any believer can carry—indwelling us with the Holy Spirit from the moment of salvation, marking us as part of God's kingdom.

As we delve deeper, it becomes evident that this indwelling of the Holy Spirit is just the beginning. Jesus Himself promised that His followers would be **Empowered Through the Holy Spirit**, a promise that extends beyond the initial salvation experience to equip us with the power to perform miracles and spread the gospel effectively. This empowerment is described as being "clothed with power from on high," a clear biblical mandate for all believers to seek the baptism of the Holy Spirit, which enhances our capability to act under the mantle of Christ with greater authority and spiritual power.

While every Christian shares this universal mantle, the New Testament also acknowledges the existence of more specific roles or **Mantles in the New Covenant**. These are not as commonly bestowed as the universal mantle of Christ but are crucial for fulfilling specialized tasks within God's plan. These specific **Mantle Assignments** are akin to the detailed roles we see in the Old Testament, carried by prophets and kings, yet they are adapted to the context of the new covenant, where the focus is more on spiritual service than on national or political leadership.

In carrying out these roles, accuracy is crucial. **Operating With Accuracy in the Spirit Realm** is essential for anyone called to carry a specific mantle. It requires a deep understanding of the spiritual realm, recognizing that it is populated by both divine and malevolent beings. A mantle carrier must be vigilant, ensuring their actions and spiritual engagements are governed by God's directives, not by human ambition or misguided spiritual warfare.

This understanding prompts us to build spiritual platforms sturdy enough to support the weight of such mantles. **The one who is called has to build the kind of platform that a mantle can sit on**, involving rigorous spiritual discipline and a deep commitment to biblical truth. This platform is constructed from a life of integrity, scriptural obedience, and continual spiritual growth.

To maintain doctrinal purity, we must engage in constant **Discernment and Doctrinal Purity**, evaluating our beliefs and spiritual experiences against the truth of Scripture. This scrutiny ensures that our ministry and personal walk with God remain pure and powerful, devoid of the corruption that can arise from spiritual deception or misinterpretation.

For effective ministry, it is imperative to stay within the **Spiritual Law of Agreement**, where the Holy Spirit's activities in our lives align seamlessly with Scripture. This alignment acts as a safeguard, protecting us from spiritual error and enhancing our effectiveness in ministry by ensuring that our actions reflect God's will as revealed in the Bible.

Finally, as ministers of the gospel and carriers of God's mantle, whether universal or specific, we must commit to **Living and Ministering Within Scriptural Boundaries**. This commitment involves preaching the gospel, performing acts of service, and engaging in spiritual warfare in ways that strictly adhere to biblical instructions, avoiding the extremes that lead either to fanaticism or ineffectiveness.

REFLECTIVE QUESTIONS

1. How does understanding the mantle of Christ affect your view of your spiritual identity and mission?
2. What steps can you take to ensure that you are 'clothed with power from on high' as Jesus instructed?
3. In what ways can you discern and ensure that your spiritual experiences align with Scripture?

4. How can the church today benefit from recognizing both universal and specific mantles?
5. What can be done to cultivate a biblical understanding of spiritual operations among believers, particularly those new to the faith?

ACTIONABLE STEPS

- **Cultivate a Relationship with the Holy Spirit**: Engage daily in prayer and Scripture study to deepen your connection with the Holy Spirit, ensuring your spiritual experiences are grounded in biblical truth.
- **Equip Yourself with Knowledge**: Participate in Bible studies or theological courses that focus on the operation of the Holy Spirit and the use of spiritual gifts, to better understand and operate within your spiritual mantle.
- **Engage in Faithful Ministry**: Actively seek opportunities to use your spiritual gifts within the church and community, always aiming to edify others and extend the kingdom of God as empowered by the Holy Spirit.

JOURNALING **Prompt**

Reflect on your experiences with the Holy Spirit. How have these moments affirmed or challenged your understanding of being 'clothed with Christ'? What steps will you take to align more closely with the biblical model of operating under the mantle of Christ?

CHAPTER 5

PREPARATION FOR A MANTLE: PURSUIT

As you walk this path, remember it is your diligent pursuit of God's presence and the mentor He has placed in your life that prepares you for the mantle you seek to carry. Trust that He is molding you through every challenge, teaching you through every setback, and strengthening you with each step forward.

"But you, be strong and do not let your hands be weak, for your work shall be rewarded!" - 2 Chronicles 15:7 NKJV

In our journey through the Scriptures and the teachings handed down through the generations, we are reminded of the profound journey one must undertake to be worthy of a spiritual mantle. Understanding this path is not merely about assuming a role; it's about embodying a divine calling that shapes your very existence and the lives of those you touch. This chapter, "Preparation for a Mantle: Pursuit," serves as a guide for those called to such a significant undertaking.

A critical component in this journey is the **Close Association with the Mantle Carrier**. This is not a casual mentorship but a profound connection that immerses you in the life and spirit of the one who currently carries the mantle. Such relationships are built on trust, respect, and a mutual recognition of the divine purpose at work. It's here in this sacred space that the mantle begins to find its next bearer.

Equally important is **Living in the Mentor's Environment**. By sharing in the daily life and challenges of the mantle carrier, you are not just observing but actively participating in the rhythms and rituals that define this holy calling. This proximity allows you to see the mantle not just as an abstract concept but as a living, breathing reality that demands everything from those it chooses.

As you are drawn into this world, you find yourself under the **Constant Influence** of your mentor. Day by day, you absorb lessons both spoken and unspoken. It's in these moments that the mantle begins to weave itself into your being, preparing you for the day when it might rest upon your shoulders.

The pursuit of a mantle is marked by an **Intentional Pursuit**. This pursuit is a conscious, deliberate action that spans the entirety of your relationship with your mentor. It is not a passive waiting but an active engagement, marked by a hunger to absorb every lesson, every correction, and every nuance of the spiritual life you aspire to inherit.

At the heart of this journey is the **Passing of the Mantle**, a moment of profound spiritual and existential significance. This act is not a simple transfer of responsibility; it is a sacred ritual that affirms God's choice and your readiness to step into a role ordained by the divine. This moment is the culmination of years of preparation, prayer, and dedication.

Throughout this process, you will face **Testing and Commitment**. These tests are not arbitrary but are designed to reveal the depth of your commitment and the purity of your spirit. Just as Elisha demonstrated his readiness by sacrificing his oxen, so too must you prove that you are ready to leave behind your former life and step fully into the role God has prepared for you.

This leads us to the necessity of **Sacrifice and Renunciation**. The path to carrying a mantle is paved with the things you must be willing to give up. This isn't just about physical or material sacrifices but about a willingness to let go of your previous identity and the expectations that come with it.

Your journey is also defined by **Spiritual Readiness and Desire**. It is essential that this desire to serve and lead is not fleeting but is a deep-seated part of who you are. This readiness involves a maturity and wisdom that can only be gained through prolonged exposure to the spiritual teachings and practices that will form the foundation of your ministry.

Understanding and respecting the **Power of the Mantle** is crucial. You must approach this role with a sense of awe and reverence, recognizing that you are stepping into a position of spiritual authority that has significant implications for both yourself and those you will lead.

Finally, the foundation of all these traits is **Servanthood as Foundation**. True leadership in the spiritual realm is marked not by power or authority but by humility and service. Your ability to serve joyfully and selflessly, even in roles that may seem menial or unnoticed, is what prepares you to carry the mantle with honor and integrity.

REFLECTIVE QUESTIONS

1. What specific actions have you taken to foster a close relationship with a spiritual mentor?
2. How have you integrated the lessons from your mentor's environment into your daily spiritual practices?

3. In what ways have you demonstrated a commitment to pursuing the mantle you seek?
4. What sacrifices have you made in your pursuit of a spiritual calling?
5. How do you balance the demands of servanthood with the aspirations of leadership?

ACTIONABLE STEPS

Cultivate a deeper relationship with your spiritual mentor through regular engagement and active listening.

Equip yourself with the necessary spiritual disciplines that support a life of service and pursuit of a mantle.

Engage in community activities that reflect the values and teachings of your mentor, enhancing your visibility and influence within your spiritual community.

JOURNALING **Prompt**

Reflect on a moment when you felt a deep connection with your spiritual path or mentor. How did this moment clarify your pursuit of the mantle? Describe the emotions and revelations that came from this experience.

CHAPTER 6
THE TRANSFER OF
THE CALL

Be steady in your faith and persistent in your spiritual pursuits. Even when the journey is long and the tasks seem overwhelming, remember that the most profound transformations often require a commitment that transcends ordinary expectations. Stay focused, keep your eyes on the eternal purpose, and trust that God equips those He calls.

2 Kings 2:10 NKJV"And he said, Thou hast asked a hard thing: nevertheless, if thou see me when I am taken from thee, it shall be so unto thee; but if not, it shall not be so."

As we delve into Chapter 6, "The Transfer of the Call," we are invited to witness a profoundly sacred moment between Elijah and Elisha, a moment that encapsulates not only a **miraculous crossing** of the Jordan River but also the pivotal passing of a prophetic mantle. Imagine standing there as Elijah wraps his mantle, strikes the water, and the river parts, allowing them both to cross on dry ground. This act was more than a display of divine power; it was a preparation for the transition of spiritual authority.

At the river's edge, as they prepared to part ways, Elijah turns to Elisha with a significant question that tests the depth of his protégé's spiritual ambition and readiness. Elisha's response, to ask for a **double portion of Elijah's spirit**, is telling of his desire not merely to continue Elijah's work but to excel in it, to reach further in the service of God. This wasn't about personal power but about amplifying the impact of God's work on earth.

Elijah's conditional promise that Elisha would receive what he asked for only if he witnessed his departure introduces a pivotal lesson about spiritual inheritance. The **conditional promise** highlights that spiritual gifts and callings require not just desire but preparedness to see and seize divine moments. It underscores that the transfer of a spiritual mantle is not automatic; it demands acute spiritual perception and presence.

As they walked and talked, a **chariot of fire** appeared, creating a divine spectacle that physically separated the two men. Elisha's reaction to Elijah's ascent into heaven is a mixture of reverence and resolve; he tears his clothes in mourning, yet also recognizes the gravity of the moment. Picking up Elijah's mantle that fell from the sky, Elisha approaches the Jordan, strikes the water, and asks, **"Where is the Lord God of Elijah?"**. As the waters part for him as well, it confirms his succession and marks the beginning of his ministry under a double portion of anointing.

The entire sequence is fraught with lessons about the nature of spiritual leadership and the **test of faith** that every potential leader must endure. It is not the dramatic manifestations of power that define a true leader but the quiet, consistent willingness to serve and follow through on God's call.

This passage also teaches us about the **spiritual preparation** necessary for those who would take up such a mantle. Elisha had to learn to set aside personal ambitions to fully embrace the responsibilities that come with divine anointing. Such preparation often involves unseen sacrifices and choices that align one's life with God's purposes, far beyond what bystanders might understand.

Reflecting on this, we understand the continuity of divine work through generations, a **legacy and continuity** that is not broken but rather bolstered by each faithful servant who takes up the mantle. Elisha's fulfillment of the prophetic role is a vibrant testament to God's sovereign orchestration and the faithfulness of those He calls.

However, the acquisition of a mantle is not without significant cost. As Elijah hinted and Elisha would learn, the **cost of ministry** can be high. Those who bear great anointing are often required to lead lives not of comfort but of constant spiritual discipline and surrender.

As you, the reader, explore this narrative, consider what it means to carry forward a legacy that is not your own but one that has been passed down through the ages. The stories of Elijah and Elisha are not just historical accounts but are active invitations to each of us to consider how we might respond when asked, "What shall I do for you before I am taken from you?" This is the essence of spiritual inheritance — it is both a gift and a grave responsibility.

REFLECTIVE QUESTIONS

1. What personal ambitions might you need to set aside to fully embrace the responsibilities that come with a divine calling?
2. How can you develop spiritual perception to

recognize and seize your divine moments as
Elisha did?

3. In what ways can you prepare yourself to inherit a
spiritual mantle or leadership role within your
community or spiritual circle?

4. How does the story of Elijah and Elisha inspire you to
think about legacy and continuity in your own life's
work?

5. What are the potential costs of spiritual leadership,
and how can you prepare to meet them?

Actionable Steps

Cultivate a deeper prayer life to enhance your spiritual
readiness and perception, similar to how Elisha prepared to
receive Elijah's mantle.

Equip yourself with knowledge and wisdom by studying the
lives and legacies of spiritual leaders you admire, understanding
the sacrifices they made and the disciplines they practiced.

Engage in activities that build your spiritual resilience and
ability to handle divine assignments, such as fasting, meditative
prayer, and prolonged periods of biblical study.

JOURNALING **Prompt**

Reflect on the question Elijah posed to Elisha: "Ask what I
shall do for thee, before I be taken away from thee." If you were
in Elisha's shoes, what would you ask for in your spiritual journey, and why? Consider what this reveals about your priorities
and spiritual ambitions.

CHAPTER 7
QUALIFIED TO ASK

In the pursuit of a spiritual mantle, **determination** and **faithfulness** are your guiding lights. It is not enough to simply desire; you must actively engage in the process God has laid out, much like Elisha did under Elijah's mentorship. Embrace the journey, knowing that the pursuit of greatness in God's kingdom is paved with steadfastness and devotion.

James 1:12 (NKJV) "Blessed is the man who endures temptation; for when he has been approved, he will receive the crown of life which the Lord has promised to those who love Him."

In our exploration of "Qualified to Ask," we dive deep into the conditions and spiritual diligence that positioned Elisha to inherit a significant prophetic role from Elijah. Elisha's journey was not merely about proximity to greatness but was defined by his unwavering **dedication and service**, which set the foundation for his bold request. The **consistent faithfulness** that Elisha demonstrated was pivotal; he wasn't just present—he was actively engaged, serving Elijah in a capacity that transcended mere duty, venturing into the realm of spiritual sonship. This deep commitment underscores a critical lesson for us: true spiritual inheritance stems from more than desire—it requires proven fidelity.

Elisha's request for a "double portion" wasn't born out of a desire for power but from a place of wanting to fully embody and continue Elijah's mission. This was not about personal gain but about ensuring that the spiritual and communal work Elijah began would not only continue but expand. The request for a **double portion** reflects a profound understanding of spiritual succession, where the spiritual son aims not just to match but to magnify the impact of his predecessor.

Through the text, we see that this transfer was not automatic; it was a divine transaction marked by miraculous confirmations. As Elisha takes up Elijah's mantle and parts the Jordan, we witness a **miraculous confirmation** of his new role. This act was a tangible sign that the spiritual authority Elijah wielded was now Elisha's to bear. This transfer and the subsequent miracles performed by Elisha—**twice as many as Elijah**—reinforce the potency of divine selection and the fulfillment of a spiritual promise.

The concept of **spiritual authority** being transferred through such a divine endorsement challenges us to consider how we perceive and engage with spiritual succession. It isn't about titles or human appointment but about a God-ordained passing of mantle which is evident through the continuation and expansion of God's work.

Understanding the **criteria for succession** is vital. Elisha's life exemplifies that one's personal ambitions must align with divine assignments. His life was not his own; his actions and goals were intricately tied to fulfilling a divine purpose that was established long before he stepped into his prophetic role.

Reflecting on this, the miracles themselves—both Elijah's and Elisha's—serve as markers of their prophetic authenticity and authority. The **role of miracles** in their ministries was not just about wonder but were signs of God's active presence and confirmation of His word through His prophets.

As readers and followers of Christ, the recognition of such spiritual succession in our own lives requires discernment and a heart attuned to God's timing and will. The **recognition of spiritual succession** within the community, as seen when the sons of the prophets acknowledged Elisha's new role, is crucial for communal spiritual health and continuity.

In your own spiritual walk, consider how mentorship and discipleship play roles in shaping your spiritual identity and capacity. The relationship between Elijah and Elisha illustrates the transformative power of **spiritual mentorship** where wisdom, power, and responsibility are passed down through close relational ties.

We are reminded that God's plans are providential. The story of Elisha shows us that **divine providence** plays a crucial role in preparing and equipping those called to lead. As you step into or grow within your own calling, remember that God is actively preparing the way for you, supplying not just opportunities but also the spiritual authority needed to fulfill His purposes.

Lastly, the lasting impact of a spiritual leader like Elisha teaches us about **legacy and impact**. His life was a testament to the enduring power of faithful service to God and provides a model for us to emulate. Whether you are called to lead many or influence a few, the depth of your commitment to God's calling is what will define your spiritual legacy.

REFLECTIVE QUESTIONS

1. How does Elisha's journey challenge your current approach to spiritual growth and pursuit?
2. In what ways can you deepen your commitment to serve those God has placed in your life as leaders?
3. What aspects of Elisha's request for a double portion resonate with your personal spiritual ambitions?
4. How do you see the role of miracles in the context of spiritual authority and succession?
5. What steps can you take to ensure your spiritual pursuits align more closely with God's overarching plans?

ACTIONABLE STEPS

1. **Cultivate a deeper relationship with spiritual mentors** by regularly engaging in meaningful conversations about faith and calling.
2. **Equip yourself with knowledge** of the biblical examples of succession and mentorship to understand the responsibilities and blessings associated with them.
3. **Engage in acts of service** that demonstrate your commitment to your community and to God, mirroring Elisha's service to Elijah.

Journaling Prompt

Reflect on the question: "What does it mean to me to ask for a double portion in my life?" Consider the responsibilities that come with such a request and journal about how you can prepare yourself to possibly receive and honor such an anointment.

≈

MANTLES PAST AND PRESENT OFFICIAL WORKBOOK

_____
_____
_____
_____
_____
_____
_____
_____
_____
_____
_____
_____
_____
_____
_____
_____
_____
_____
_____
_____
_____
_____
_____
_____
_____
_____
_____
_____
_____
_____
_____

CHAPTER 8
THE COST OF SAYING YES

Embrace your divine calling with courage and faithfulness.
When you accept God's mission for your life, you are stepping
into a realm where heavenly support and earthly challenges
coexist. Trust in God's provision and protection as you move
forward in obedience.

**James 1:12 (NKJV) "Blessed is the man who endures
temptation; for when he has been approved, he will receive
the crown of life which the Lord has promised to those who
love Him."**

"The Cost of Saying Yes," we delve into the intricacies of
Elisha's early days as a prophet, highlighting the
immediate challenges and the **perseverance** required
when stepping into a divine role. Elisha's encounter with
mockery shortly after his initial miracle reveals a significant
aspect of spiritual leadership—the inevitability of **persecution**
and **opposition**. This confrontation at Bethel, where he was
mocked by youths and responded with a curse, is not just about

the challenge of being derided but also underscores the weighty responsibility of carrying a prophetic mantle.

The episode teaches us that accepting a mantle from God is not without its trials. These challenges are not mere obstacles; they are opportunities to affirm one's dedication to God's path. This incident is a profound illustration of the **serious consequences** of disrespecting God's anointed and the protective authority granted to those who serve Him faithfully.

Moreover, the chapter emphasizes that the **responsibility** of a spiritual mantle involves more than just performing miracles or leading people; it extends to **correcting or completing unfinished divine tasks**. This could be seen as Elijah left behind some assignments uncompleted, which Elisha had to take up, demonstrating that part of carrying a mantle involves finishing the work started by predecessors.

Elisha's journey also exemplifies the **personal cost** of saying yes to God's call. It involves not only public ministry but also private battles with discouragement and societal rejection. The story of Elisha at Bethel reflects the broader biblical principle that those who wish to live a godly life will face persecution.

REFLECTIVE QUESTIONS

1. How does Elisha's response to mockery at Bethel shape your understanding of the authority and responsibilities of a spiritual mantle?
2. What personal sacrifices might you need to prepare for if called to a similar position of spiritual authority?
3. In what ways can you better support those in leadership to help them fulfill their divine mandates?

4. How does the concept of completing unfinished tasks from predecessors apply to your spiritual or ministerial life?
5. What lessons can you draw from the balance Elisha had to maintain between spiritual authority and personal humility?

ACTIONABLE STEPS

1. **Cultivate resilience and spiritual depth** by studying the lives of biblical figures who faced opposition and persevered.
2. **Equip yourself with a thorough understanding of biblical doctrine** related to spiritual authority and the prophetic office to handle responsibilities wisely.
3. **Engage in supportive relationships** within your faith community to foster an environment where leaders can perform their duties without undue hardship.

JOURNALING **Prompt**

Reflect on a time when you faced opposition or mockery for your faith or moral stance. How did you handle it? What might you learn from Elisha's example that could help you in handling similar situations in the future? Write down your thoughts and any scripture that comes to mind that could fortify you for future challenges.

∽

THE COST OF SAYING YES

CHAPTER 9

SPIRITUAL FATHERS AND SONS

Lean on God's grace to guide you through life's complexities. Let His wisdom fill you as He uses those He has placed in your life for your growth and preparation.

"For though you might have ten thousand instructors in Christ, yet you do not have many fathers; for in Christ Jesus I have begotten you through the gospel." - 1 Corinthians 4:15 NKJV

In this chapter, I delve into the profound dynamics between Elijah and Elisha, exploring the essence of spiritual fatherhood, which far transcends the typical roles of mentorship or life coaching that we often encounter. This relationship, deeply rooted in the spiritual tradition, was not merely about transferring knowledge or skills but about fostering deep personal and spiritual growth. **The profound declaration "My father, my father!"** by Elisha, as he witnessed Elijah being taken up into heaven in a whirlwind, encapsulates the deep emotional and spiritual bond that had formed between them.

This wasn't a casual farewell; it was a poignant acknowledgment of Elijah's role as much more than a mentor—he was a spiritual father to Elisha.

Spiritual fatherhood is crucial for the transfer of a mantle; it is about imparting not just skills and knowledge but also character and spiritual depth. This depth is essential for handling divine assignments with integrity and effectiveness. The relationship between Elijah and Elisha is a perfect illustration of how spiritual parenting prepares the successor not only to receive the mantle but to thrive under its weight and to further the kingdom's work with greater impact.

Furthermore, spiritual parenting provides **corrective guidance** which is pivotal in spiritual growth. Unlike mentors or coaches who may opt for a more hands-off approach, a spiritual parent delves into the nitty-gritty of personal and spiritual issues. They correct, guide, and sometimes rebuke, which is essential for maturation in the faith. This depth of interaction ensures that the spiritual child grows under careful, loving scrutiny, much like a craftsman meticulously shaping a precious artifact.

One of the unique aspects of this dynamic is that **you do not choose your spiritual father—you discover him.** This discovery is not based on convenience or charisma but is a divinely orchestrated alignment that God sets in place to ensure you receive the nurturing necessary to fulfill your calling. This realization has profound implications for how we engage with spiritual authority and submit to the guidance of those God places over us.

The role of a spiritual father, therefore, is to prepare you for your own journey of faith, ensuring that **the mantle you may one day carry** is borne with wisdom, humility, and power. It's about raising you from spiritual infancy to maturity, ensuring that when the time comes for you to step into your calling, you are not only ready but fully equipped to walk in it with authority and grace.

In this relationship, the spiritual father focuses more on **character than on gifting.** It's easy to become enamored with the gifts and anointings God places on our lives, but without a strong character, those gifts can lead us astray. Elijah's mentoring of Elisha emphasized character-building over the prophetic acts themselves, which ensured that Elisha would not only inherit Elijah's mantle but would do so with the integrity and moral fortitude necessary to handle it rightly.

This nurturing process is crucial because it also involves preparing the spiritual child to handle both the responsibilities and the trials they will face. As Elijah prepared Elisha for the realities of spiritual warfare and prophetic ministry, he was also instilling in him the resilience needed to withstand the challenges that come with such a calling.

Moreover, this chapter illuminates the necessity for spiritual sons and daughters to **recognize and honor the weight of their inheritance**—not just the power and authority of a spiritual mantle but also the responsibility to carry forward the legacy of their spiritual forebears. This recognition ensures that the transfer of spiritual authority from one generation to the next is marked not only by continuity but also by a deepening and expansion of the divine work begun by those who came before us.

As we explore these dynamics, we see that the role of a spiritual father or mother is complex and layered, requiring a depth of spiritual maturity that can only be developed through a life lived in close communion with God and His people. This chapter aims to unpack these layers, offering you, the reader, a roadmap to understanding and perhaps even stepping into the role of a spiritual parent or child in your own spiritual journey.

REFLECTIVE QUESTIONS

1. How does the concept of spiritual fatherhood affect your view of spiritual authority and mentorship?
2. In what ways can spiritual parents impact the readiness and effectiveness of their spiritual children in ministry?
3. What qualities should you look for in a spiritual father or mother, and how can these relationships be fostered within your community?
4. How does the relationship between Elijah and Elisha inspire you to pursue or provide spiritual mentorship?
5. What steps can you take to ensure that your spiritual relationships are rooted in genuine love and commitment rather than convenience or necessity?

ACTIONABLE STEPS

1. **Cultivate deeper spiritual relationships** by identifying and connecting with potential spiritual mentors who exhibit the qualities of true spiritual fatherhood or motherhood.
2. **Equip yourself with knowledge and understanding** of what it means to be a spiritual father or mother, studying biblical examples and seeking guidance from church leaders.
3. **Engage actively in your spiritual community**, offering to mentor younger believers or seeking out mentorship for yourself, emphasizing the importance

of character development over talent or skill enhancement.

JOURNALING Prompt

Reflect on the relationships in your life that have had a formative impact on your spiritual development. Consider how a spiritual father or mother could further enhance your growth. What qualities would you seek in such a relationship? Write about your thoughts and how you might take steps to foster such significant relationships in your life.

∼

CHAPTER 10

PORTRAIT OF A SPIRITUAL FATHER

Be encouraged by knowing that in your spiritual journey, you are
never alone. God provides mentors—spiritual fathers and
mothers—who guide us, not just through the easy parts, but
through challenging seasons. They impart wisdom, not only in
our spiritual gifts but also in character and governance, ensuring
that we grow to reflect Christ in all aspects of life.

**"For though you might have ten thousand instructors in
Christ, yet you do not have many fathers; for in Christ Jesus I
have begotten you through the gospel." - 1 Corinthians
4:15, NKJV**

In my journey through spiritual growth and ministry, I've
been profoundly shaped by the presence and mentorship
of Dr. Lester Sumrall, a true **spiritual father** whose impact
goes beyond mere teaching. He emphasized the importance of
character and self-governance, which are foundational for
anyone called to serve in God's kingdom. This deep nurturing is

essential, as it focuses on building lasting qualities that sustain one's ministry.

The role of a spiritual father is crucial, not just for imparting skills or anointing, but for the deep-rooted development of one's personal and spiritual life. Dr. Sumrall taught me that spiritual parenting involves more than just addressing spiritual gifts; it includes a comprehensive cultivation of character. This approach ensures that the spiritual sons and daughters are prepared not only to handle the gifts of the Spirit but also to face various challenges in life and ministry with integrity and wisdom.

A **personal touch in ministry** was evident in how Dr. Sumrall dealt with those he mentored. He could see beyond my immediate mistakes or the surface level issues and focus on what was necessary for long-term growth. His commitment to my growth was not limited to times of comfort but extended deeply into periods of personal struggle, making sure that I, and many others, did not falter in our calls due to temporary setbacks or wounds inflicted by life's battles.

I remember vividly how Dr. Sumrall stood by me during some of my lowest moments, embodying the **commitment to restoration** that every spiritual leader should have. His willingness to listen, correct, and guide me through complex issues was invaluable. His mentorship was not only about guiding me through the easy parts of life but also standing with me in the trenches, helping me navigate through the painful and confusing times.

Corrective love is a hallmark of true spiritual fatherhood. Dr. Sumrall was never shy to correct me when I was wrong, a quality that might seem harsh to some but is deeply necessary for those who seek to grow spiritually and personally. His corrections were always from a place of love—a desire to see me, and others like me, thrive and not just survive.

Moreover, Dr. Sumrall's teaching on **teaching self-governance** was pivotal. He believed that a minister must learn to govern themselves before they can effectively lead others. This teaching has helped me realize that self-governance in one's spiritual and personal life is crucial for ministry. It prevents the pitfalls that come from unchecked behaviors and aligns one's daily actions with the will of God.

Through his life, Dr. Sumrall also demonstrated the **importance of character over gifts**. It is easy to become enamored with the spiritual gifts one might possess, but without a solid character, those gifts can lead to pride and ultimately to one's downfall. Dr. Sumrall's focus was always on building the character of his spiritual children so that they could handle God's anointing with humility and integrity.

In our relationship, he also highlighted the importance of **openness to difficult conversations**, especially around topics like deliverance and spiritual warfare. These conversations, though tough, were necessary for shedding light on misunderstood aspects of ministry and for preventing the mishandling of spiritual gifts.

Reflecting on his legacy, the **legacy of spiritual fatherhood** is perhaps one of the most profound lessons. Dr. Sumrall's life was a testament to the enduring impact a spiritual father can have, not just on his immediate spiritual children but on generations to come. His teachings and life continue to influence many across the world, proving that the work of a spiritual father extends far beyond their earthly existence.

Lastly, **celebration of spiritual sonship** is something I hold dear. It is about honoring the relationship that has helped shape you into who you are. It involves acknowledging and respecting the role a spiritual father has played in your life, which in turn, helps perpetuate the culture of honor and respect in the body of Christ.

. . .

REFLECTIVE QUESTIONS

1. How can the role of a spiritual father impact one's personal and ministry growth?
2. In what ways have you experienced or witnessed the corrective love of a spiritual mentor?
3. What are the key characteristics that distinguish a true spiritual father from a mere mentor or coach?
4. How can one cultivate a character that sustains the anointing and gifts given by God?
5. Reflect on a time when a spiritual father or mother's guidance helped you navigate a difficult period in your life.

ACTIONABLE STEPS

Cultivate: Develop a daily habit of self-reflection to assess areas of personal character that need growth or alignment with biblical principles.

Equip: Engage in a mentorship relationship, either by seeking a spiritual father/mother or by offering to mentor someone else, focusing on character development and spiritual maturity.

Engage: Actively participate in a community of faith where experiences and wisdom can be shared, enhancing mutual growth and understanding.

JOURNALING Prompt

Reflect on your relationships with spiritual authorities in your life. How have these relationships shaped your faith and character? Write about a specific instance where a spiritual father or mother profoundly impacted your spiritual journey.

～

PORTRAIT OF A SPIRITUAL FATHER

CHAPTER 11
THE VITAL ROLE OF A PASTOR

Let me encourage you today by reminding you of the importance of submission to spiritual authority. God's plan for us is often revealed through the care, correction, and love of a pastor. When we embrace the direction provided by our pastor, we open ourselves to growth, wisdom, and alignment with God's purpose. Remember that even when correction feels uncomfortable, it is an act of love designed to guide us toward fulfilling our divine calling.

Proverbs 12:1 (NKJV) "Whoever loves instruction loves knowledge, But he who hates correction is stupid."

Every person, no matter their calling or position, needs a pastor. This truth became incredibly real to me as I walked with my pastor, Billy Joe Daugherty, for nearly three decades. He played an essential role in my life, guiding me through correction and helping me grow. **God intended for each of us to be under pastoral leadership**—someone to speak into our lives, challenge us, and steer us away from potential dangers.

Some may believe that pastors hold a lesser role than prophets or apostles, but that is not biblical. Everyone, no matter their spiritual office, requires the stabilizing presence of a pastor.

A pastor's job is not only to encourage but also to correct. There were times when Pastor Billy Joe lovingly addressed things in my life that needed to change. For instance, one day he sat me down and pointed out that while my teachings were correct in principle, **adjusting my delivery would help avoid unnecessary conflict**. He emphasized that how we say things in ministry matters. That conversation challenged my pride, and at first, I resisted internally. I thought people could figure it out for themselves, but over time, I realized he was right. The goal was to reach people, not defend my preferences.

Correction can feel intrusive, but a true pastor's heart is filled with love and the desire to remove obstacles in our path before they become stumbling blocks. Pastor Billy Joe showed me that **a pastor's correction is an act of love and honor**, even when it feels difficult to accept. The lesson I learned was that growth requires humility. Pride often prevents us from seeing what we need to change, but when we listen to our pastors, we gain the opportunity to grow and flourish in ways we never expected.

I can recall another pivotal moment when Pastor Billy Joe gave me advice on my teaching style. His gentle guidance helped me see that **changing the way we communicate can make a message more effective**. This was a humbling experience, as I initially resisted the advice, thinking I knew best. But over time, I understood that he wasn't trying to control my ministry; he was helping me become more effective in my calling. I eventually came to see that this kind of correction wasn't about suppressing my voice but about refining it for God's purposes.

Reflecting on my journey, I see how vital **the relationship with a pastor is for every believer**. It is foundational, a covering that provides accountability, wisdom, and protection. My relationship with Pastor Billy Joe spanned nearly 30 years, and in that time, he continually steered me in the right direction, helping me avoid pitfalls that could have derailed my ministry.

One of the greatest lessons I learned from Pastor Billy Joe was that **embracing pastoral correction is a pathway to growth.** We can't afford to allow pride to hinder us from receiving the counsel we need. Spiritual growth requires us to remain teachable and open to correction, even when it stings. Those moments of correction, though difficult, became some of the most defining moments of my life and ministry.

In summary, **the role of a pastor is critical in every believer's life**. They are God's appointed shepherds, called to nurture, correct, and guide us toward the fulfillment of His purposes. We honor God when we submit to our pastors, trusting that they are operating out of love for us and concern for our spiritual growth. It is through this relationship that we are sharpened, refined, and prepared for the work of the ministry.

REFLECTIVE QUESTIONS

1. How has your relationship with a pastor impacted your spiritual growth?
2. Are there areas in your life where you resist correction? How can you be more open to receiving guidance?
3. In what ways can you honor the role of a pastor in your life, especially when correction feels difficult?
4. Have you experienced a time when pastoral advice helped you avoid a mistake? What did you learn from that?
5. How does humility play a role in accepting correction from your spiritual leaders?

. . .

Actionable Steps

Cultivate an open heart toward pastoral correction, understanding that it is an act of love meant to guide you.

Equip yourself by regularly seeking feedback from your pastor on areas where you can grow spiritually or in ministry.

Engage with your pastor's teachings, trusting that God has placed them in your life for your spiritual development and protection.

Journaling Prompt

Reflect on a time when you resisted correction from your pastor or spiritual leader. How did that experience shape your understanding of humility and growth? Write about how you can better position yourself to receive correction with an open heart, trusting that it will lead to spiritual maturity.

THE VITAL ROLE OF A PASTOR

70

CHAPTER 12

ELISHA AND ELIJAH: THE UNFOLDING JOURNEY

Stay faithful to the process, and you will see how God works through the mentorship of spiritual fathers and mothers to prepare you for the mantle He has reserved for you. Your journey might involve cutting away the old, learning God's ways, battling spiritual forces, and being entrusted with His anointing, but in each stage, He is faithful to equip you.

"For I know the thoughts that I think toward you, says the Lord, thoughts of peace and not of evil, to give you a future and a hope." — Jeremiah 29:11 (NKJV)

The relationship between Elijah and Elisha presents us with a profound picture of the spiritual father-son dynamic and the process of receiving a mantle. Elisha's journey began with his refusal to leave Elijah's side, marking the importance of loyalty and perseverance in the process of spiritual growth. **The first key point** is that Elisha's journey started at **Gilgal, a place of cutting away the flesh.** Just as the Israelites were circumcised in Gilgal, removing the reproach of Egypt, Elisha's journey symbolizes the spiritual cutting away of selfish ambition and fleshly desires. To receive a mantle, we must first rid ourselves of personal desires that conflict with God's will.

After leaving Gilgal, Elijah and Elisha traveled to Bethel, **the second key point** in this spiritual journey. Bethel, meaning "house of God," represents the place where we **learn the ways of God**. It is in this stage of spiritual training that we walk closely with a mentor, much like Elisha did with Elijah, learning the ways of covenant, obedience, and consecration. Elisha's decision to follow Elijah from Bethel symbolizes the importance of learning directly from those who have gone before us in faith.

Their journey continued to Jericho, where **the third key point emerges: Jericho represents the place of battle**. Jericho was where the Israelites faced their first major battle in the Promised Land, and it serves as a symbol of the spiritual warfare that mantle carriers must engage in. The warfare of a mantle bearer is not an occasional fight but a constant battle against spiritual forces assigned to derail the call of God on their life. Elisha learned from Elijah the necessity of spiritual warfare and how to stand firm in the face of opposition.

Elijah and Elisha then arrived at the Jordan River, where **the fourth key point** is made clear: **the Jordan represents the anointing**. The Jordan River, which flows down from Mount Hermon, symbolizes the flow of the anointing. It was at this river that Elijah performed his last miracle before being taken to heaven, and it was here that Elisha received the double portion of Elijah's spirit. The Jordan represents the final step in the journey where the son is ready to receive and operate in the anointing of the spiritual father.

Throughout this journey, **the fifth key point** stands out: **faithfulness to the process of discipleship**. Elisha's refusal to leave Elijah, even when urged to stay behind, highlights the importance of staying committed through every stage of spiritual growth. Faithfulness is a critical factor in receiving the mantle, as it demonstrates readiness to carry the responsibility and authority that comes with it.

Elisha's journey also teaches us that **the sixth key point** is that **the mantle is not given lightly.** The process of receiving a mantle involves being tested in areas of character, faith, and perseverance. Elisha had to prove himself worthy of Elijah's mantle by showing his willingness to sacrifice, learn, fight, and endure. Spiritual authority is given to those who have been faithful through the process of preparation.

The seventh key point reminds us that **mentorship is a two-way relationship.** Elijah invested in Elisha's development, guiding him through each stage of growth, while Elisha honored Elijah by remaining teachable and loyal. This mutual commitment is essential for the transfer of spiritual mantles. Without Elijah's guidance, Elisha would not have been equipped to carry the mantle, and without Elisha's obedience, he would have missed his calling.

Spiritual warfare plays a significant role in the life of a mantle carrier, as seen in **the eighth key point: Satan assigns principalities to attack those with significant spiritual authority.** Those who carry great anointing face heightened spiritual opposition, as the enemy seeks to exploit weaknesses and derail the ministry. Elisha's training under Elijah prepared him for the spiritual battles that lay ahead, teaching us that we must be vigilant and rely on God's strength in the face of spiritual warfare.

The ninth key point is that **God honors perseverance and obedience.** Elisha's determination to follow Elijah, despite the challenges, opened the door for him to receive the double portion of Elijah's spirit. His faithfulness teaches us that God rewards those who remain committed to His call, even when the journey is difficult. Perseverance is often the key to unlocking greater levels of anointing and spiritual authority.

Finally, **the tenth key point** is that **the mantle must be passed on**. Elijah's ministry did not end with his departure; it continued through Elisha. This principle teaches us the importance of raising up the next generation of leaders to carry on the work. Mantles are meant to be transferred, ensuring that the legacy of faith continues. Elisha's ability to step into Elijah's role demonstrates the power of spiritual succession when the next generation is properly prepared and equipped.

REFLECTIVE QUESTIONS

1. In what areas of your life might God be asking you to "cut away the flesh" in order to prepare you for the next step in your spiritual journey?
2. How have you experienced learning the ways of God through a spiritual mentor or pastor?
3. What spiritual battles have you faced that have helped shape your faith, and how did you overcome them?
4. How do you stay connected to the flow of God's anointing in your life, especially during times of spiritual warfare?
5. What steps can you take to remain faithful to the process of discipleship and mentorship, even when it is challenging?

ACTIONABLE STEPS

1. **Cultivate** humility by examining your heart and asking God to reveal any areas of pride or selfish ambition that need to be cut away.
2. **Equip** yourself with the wisdom of spiritual mentors by seeking out opportunities to learn from those who have walked the path of faith before you.
3. **Engage** in spiritual warfare with confidence, knowing that God has equipped you with the strength and authority to overcome the enemy's attacks.

JOURNALING **Prompt**

Reflect on a time when you felt tested in your spiritual journey. How did that experience shape your faith, and what did you learn from it about God's faithfulness and your own perseverance? Write about how you can apply those lessons to your current season of life.

~

CHAPTER 13

A 'MANTLE TOUR' THROUGH THREE GENERATIONS

Lean into your faith, embrace your calling, and let God use you mightily. Remember that the challenges and trials you face are not merely obstacles but stepping stones to higher places in Him.

James 1:12 (NKJV): "Blessed is the man who endures temptation; for when he has been approved, he will receive the crown of life which the Lord has promised to those who love Him."

I n this chapter, I invite you to walk with me as we trace the **National Scope of the Mantle** that has significantly shaped America's spiritual landscape through the ministry of healing. This mantle, endowed with God's miraculous power, was not limited to personal achievements but permeated the national consciousness, highlighting the profound intersection of divine calling and cultural impact.

The journey of this mantle began with **Maria Woodworth-Etter**, whose ministry in the late 19th century laid the groundwork for the dramatic demonstrations of God's power that would follow. Her commitment set the stage for the mantle's progression, showcasing how divine gifts are not only inherited but cultivated through steadfast faith and resilience in the face of societal resistance. Maria's story is a vivid reminder of the foundational steps necessary for carrying such a significant anointing.

As we move through the generations, the mantle found its way to **Aimee Semple McPherson**, a dynamic figure whose innovative approaches to ministry captivated the nation. Her ability to blend the gospel's message with modern mediums exemplified how mantles can evolve to meet the times without losing their spiritual potency. Aimee's ministry was marked by a unique blend of charisma and controversy, providing a complex yet enlightening chapter in the history of this healing mantle.

The mantle's journey continued with **Kathryn Kuhlman**, who is remembered for her deep spiritual connection and the profound impact of her healing services. Kathryn's ministry highlighted the **personal trials and media relationships** that often accompany such a public figure, illustrating the dual nature of spiritual mantles that attract both divine favor and intense scrutiny. Her life teaches us the importance of maintaining focus on God's work amidst the tumult of public life.

Throughout these narratives, we observe a recurring theme of **Persecution and Public Scrutiny**, a testament to the challenges faced by those called to carry such weighty spiritual responsibilities. The public and private battles of these women underscore the **enduring impact despite opposition**, a profound legacy that continues to inspire and instruct.

Their ministries were also characterized by the **Symbolic Use of White**, representing purity and holiness, which they embraced both in attire and in the spiritual significance of their work. This visual symbolism served as a constant reminder of their divine mission and the holy standards to which they were called.

Moreover, the personal lives of these women were marked by **marital and personal trials**, which were often public and painful. Yet, these trials were part of the complex tapestry that made up their ministries, reminding us that those anointed are not immune to life's trials but are called to navigate them with grace.

The spiritual battles they faced were not just personal but involved **opposition from the spiritual realm**, with each woman confronting specific demonic strategies aimed at undermining their ministries. This aspect of their stories is particularly instructive for understanding the **warfare factor** inherent in carrying a mantle, which involves continuous spiritual vigilance and prayer.

Finally, the **common threads** in their stories, including their struggles with heart issues and their experiences with loss, reveal the personal cost of carrying such a powerful anointing. These elements underscore the reality that the anointing comes with both great power and great responsibility.

As we reflect on these stories, it becomes clear that carrying a mantle is not merely about the miracles performed but about the journey of faithfulness, endurance, and humility. This chapter invites you to consider not only the history of these great women but also the personal implications of carrying a mantle in your own life. How will you respond to the call, and what legacy will you leave for the generations that follow?

REFLECTIVE QUESTIONS

1. How does the story of Maria Woodworth-Etter inspire you to overcome societal resistance in your ministry?
2. What can you learn from Aimee Semple McPherson's ability to adapt her ministry to the needs of her time?
3. In what ways does Kathryn Kuhlman's focus on spiritual depth influence your understanding of effective ministry?
4. How do the personal trials of these women change your perception of the costs associated with spiritual callings?
5. What strategies can you adopt to protect yourself from the spiritual warfare that accompanies significant spiritual mantles?

ACTIONABLE STEPS

1. **Cultivate** a deeper understanding of the historical context of these mantles by reading more about the lives of these women beyond this chapter.
2. **Equip** yourself with the spiritual disciplines observed by these women to help navigate the challenges associated with carrying a mantle.
3. **Engage** in community discussions or forums that focus on the continuation and challenges of modern-day spiritual mantles.

Journaling Prompt

Reflect on the challenges faced by Maria, Aimee, and Kathryn. How do their stories inspire you to handle the scrutiny and pressures associated with public ministry? Write about your thoughts and how you can apply their lessons to your own life and calling.

∼

A 'MANTLE TOUR' THROUGH THREE GENERATIONS

CHAPTER 14

AMERICA'S TOP HEALING MANTLE 1ST GENERATION: MARIA WOODWORTH-ETTER

Hold firm in your faith when facing opposition, knowing that God's empowerment is perfected in our weaknesses. Stand boldly as Maria did, using your God-given gifts to fulfill His calling.

James 1:12 (NKJV) "Blessed is the man who endures temptation; for when he has been approved, he will receive the crown of life which the Lord has promised to those who love Him."

As I share the remarkable journey of Maria Woodworth-Etter, it's evident that she was not just a figure in history; she was a **pioneering Pentecostal** force whose impact is still felt today. Her early adoption of the full spectrum of spiritual gifts, including speaking in tongues, marked her as a forerunner of what many recognize as modern Pentecostalism. This legacy is particularly poignant considering the societal norms of her time, which often hindered women from taking prominent roles in ministry. Yet, Maria stood as a beacon, **overcoming opposition** with a tenacity that spoke of her deep conviction and divine calling.

Her ministry wasn't just about preaching; it was a demonstration of the **manifestation of spiritual gifts**. Each sermon and healing service was a testament to her belief that these gifts were accessible and essential for the body of Christ. This stance challenged the status quo, laying foundational beliefs that would encourage future generations to seek a similarly empowered walk with God. Moreover, her role in shaping the acceptance of **women in spiritual leadership** cannot be overstated. Through her example, she provided a blueprint for overcoming gender barriers in ministry, showing that God's call transcends human-imposed limits.

Maria's teachings on **healing as part of Christ's redemption** played a pivotal role in her ministry. She fervently believed and taught that healing was a right afforded to believers through Christ's sacrificial act, a revolutionary idea that redefined the concept of divine healing in her era. Her services were often marked by profound **visions and spiritual encounters**, which not only guided her ministry but also affirmed her calling and equipped her to handle the immense spiritual and societal pressures she faced.

Her life was a battlefield, both spiritually and culturally. Maria contended with not just the physical ailments of those she ministered to but also with **cultural and spiritual battles** that sought to discredit and disrupt her work. Her resilience in these battles was rooted in her profound spiritual life, where she engaged deeply in **private prayer and apostolic preaching**. These were not merely acts of faith but strategies of war against the principalities and powers she believed stood against her mission.

The **impact of her ministry** was not limited to the spiritual realm but was evident in the physical revitalization of communities and churches. She was tasked with reviving dying congregations and often sent to what was considered the hardest places to minister, yet she turned these challenges into testimonies of transformation. This aspect of her ministry highlighted her unique role in **making hard ground yield fruit**, preparing the way for a greater move of God wherever she went.

Through it all, Maria's journey was a powerful narrative of divine qualification. Despite her own admitted weaknesses and the immense obstacles she faced, she held fast to the conviction that if God called her, He would also make a way for her. This divine **empowerment** was evident in every aspect of her ministry, from the miraculous healings to the powerful sermons that captivated and converted many.

REFLECTIVE QUESTIONS

1. How does Maria's story inspire you to overcome cultural or societal barriers in your life?
2. What spiritual gifts do you feel are being stirred within you, and how can you develop them?
3. In what ways can you demonstrate faith and resilience in your ministry or service to others?
4. How can Maria's approach to spiritual warfare and opposition inform your own spiritual battles?
5. What lessons can you learn from Maria's experience with visions and spiritual encounters to apply to your personal walk with God?

ACTIONABLE STEPS

1. **Cultivate a robust prayer life:** Like Maria, spend time in prayer to build spiritual strength and sensitivity.
2. **Equip yourself with knowledge:** Study the Scriptures and teachings on spiritual gifts to understand and operate in them effectively.
3. **Engage in ministry opportunities:** Seek and embrace opportunities to use your gifts, even in small beginnings, to grow and learn.

JOURNALING **Prompt**

Reflect on a time when you felt called to do something outside of your comfort zone. How did you respond? What might you do differently now, inspired by Maria's example?

～

CHAPTER 15

AMERICA'S TOP HEALING MANTLE 2ND GENERATION: AIMEE SEMPLE MCPHERSON

Hold courageously to the truth that our trials prepare us for a greater destiny, enabling us to carry forth a legacy of faith and power beyond ourselves.

Hebrews 12:1 (NKJV) **"Therefore we also, since we are surrounded by so great a cloud of witnesses, let us lay aside every weight, and the sin which so easily ensnares us, and let us run with endurance the race that is set before us."**

IN OUR EXPLORATION of Aimee Semple McPherson's life, we witness a remarkable journey marked by **extraordinary faith and perseverance** amidst trials. Aimee's early encounters with Pentecostalism instilled in her a fierce desire to embrace and spread the full gospel, which included preaching, healing, and speaking in tongues. Her story is a vivid portrayal of **spiritual hunger** that refused to be satiated by the norms of her time, driving her to pursue a radical ministry path that many of her contemporaries dared not tread.

From her **youthful zeal and encounter with the Holy Spirit**, Aimee's ministry was characterized by bold moves that often placed her at the forefront of societal and spiritual battles. She didn't just dip her toes into the waters of ministry; she dove in headfirst, despite the numerous cultural and logistical obstacles that stood in her way. This included overcoming the backlash against her public ministry roles, which was particularly controversial given her gender during that era. Her ministry was not just about preaching; it was about demonstrating the power of God through **healings and public faith declarations**.

Her move across the nation in a "Gospel Car" during the 1918 Spanish flu pandemic exemplifies her **undaunted commitment to spreading the gospel**. Aimee's life was a series of stepping into the unknown and trusting God for the outcomes, illustrating her deep commitment to her divine calling. This journey was often solitary and fraught with challenges that would have discouraged a lesser spirit, but Aimee continued, fueled by a conviction that she was doing God's work.

One of the most poignant aspects of Aimee's ministry was her ability to **transform personal and societal obstacles into opportunities** for ministry. Whether it was turning a kidnapping ordeal into a testimony of faith or using her theatrical talents to draw larger crowds than many Hollywood stars of her time, Aimee's life was a testament to using one's entire being for the purposes of God. Her ministry, characterized by **dramatic and engaging sermons**, broke the mold of traditional preaching and reached people in an era where radio and film were just beginning to influence public life.

Moreover, Aimee's personal life, marked by **multiple marriages and intense scrutiny**, mirrored the tumultuous path of her public ministry. Yet, these personal trials did not deter her;

instead, they deepened her reliance on God's guidance and provision. Her life teaches us the powerful lesson that our personal and spiritual battles are not separate; they are intertwined, and victory in one area can fortify us in another.

Reflective Questions

1. What can Aimee's response to personal and public challenges teach us about resilience in our spiritual walks?
2. How does Aimee's integration of creativity in ministry inspire you to use your unique gifts for God's glory?
3. In what ways can we emulate Aimee's boldness in facing societal norms that conflict with God's call?
4. How might we better support those in ministry who are facing personal and public trials?
5. What steps can you take to incorporate more of your personal passions into your spiritual service?

Actionable Steps

1. **Cultivate a deep prayer life:** Emulate Aimee's practice of turning to prayer amidst trials to seek God's strength and guidance.
2. **Equip yourself with Scriptural truths:** Study the Bible to understand the foundations of faith that empowered Aimee to overcome great obstacles.
3. **Engage in bold witnessing:** Step out in faith to share

the gospel in creative and effective ways, as Aimee
did, even when it seems daunting.

JOURNALING **Prompt**

Reflect on a recent challenge you faced in your life. How did
you respond? Inspired by Aimee's example, how might you
approach similar challenges in the future with faith and
creativity?

~

CHAPTER 16

AMERICA'S TOP HEALING MANTLE 3RD GENERATION: KATHRYN KUHLMAN

Let your heart be encouraged by the truth that God can transform our deepest weaknesses into profound strengths, redeeming our past for a powerful testimony of His grace.

2 Corinthians 12:9 (NKJV) "And He said to me, 'My grace is sufficient for you, for My strength is made perfect in weakness.' Therefore most gladly I will rather boast in my infirmities, that the power of Christ may rest upon me."

Kathryn Kuhlman's life story unfolds as a testament to the transformative power of faith and the real impact of divine calling. The narrative of her ministry demonstrates a profound journey of **spiritual renewal and healing authority**, which she embraced after overcoming personal and professional adversities. Her initial encounter with the divine presence at a young age instilled a deep-seated passion for the gospel, which she pursued with **unyielding tenacity** despite the societal norms that often hindered women from such callings.

Kathryn's ministry, marked by her distinctively gentle yet powerful stage presence, showcased her unique ability to foster an atmosphere where **miracles seemed to flow spontaneously**. Her services were characterized not just by the preaching of the Word, but by visible, often instant, **healings**, confirming the presence of the Holy Spirit working through her.

Her story is also one of personal struggle and **redemption**— Kathryn's early marital choices led to years of hardship, yet these experiences shaped her into a vessel ready to be wholly used by God. It was at a pivotal moment of complete surrender at Aimee Semple McPherson's gravesite that Kathryn's new phase of ministry was birthed, marked by a deeper reliance on God's power rather than human effort.

Kathryn's meetings were not merely gatherings; they were spiritual experiences where many encountered God's healing power firsthand. The legacy of her ministry is encapsulated in her unwavering declaration that it was not by her power but by the Holy Spirit that lives were transformed—**a testament to divine strength manifesting in human weakness.**

REFLECTIVE QUESTIONS

1. How does Kathryn's journey inspire us to pursue our divine calling despite personal failures and societal challenges?
2. What lessons can we learn from Kathryn's experience that faith and genuine surrender can lead to profound spiritual encounters?
3. In what ways can Kathryn's ministry encourage us to trust in God's timing and His ultimate plan for our lives?

4. How can her legacy challenge us to seek a deeper filling of the Holy Spirit in our own ministries or daily lives?

5. What can we draw from Kathryn's story to help others in their spiritual walk, especially those who feel disqualified by their past?

ACTIONABLE STEPS

1. **Cultivate a heart of worship:** Dedicate time daily to seek God's presence and power, allowing His Spirit to fill and refresh you as it did Kathryn.

2. **Equip yourself with knowledge of God's Word:** Regularly study the Scriptures to understand the basis of faith and healing, which were central to Kathryn's ministry.

3. **Engage in compassionate ministry:** Look for opportunities to serve and pray for others, offering God's love and healing as Kathryn did, emphasizing His power over our limitations.

JOURNALING Prompt

Reflect on a time when you felt your weakness was too great to be used by God. How does Kathryn's story shift your perspective on God's ability to use your weaknesses for His glory? Write about how you can apply this understanding in your current circumstances or ministry.

CHAPTER 17

'FOLLOW ME, AS I FOLLOW CHRIST'

Be encouraged, dear reader, that your journey in faith is never solitary. As you step forward, remember that the path has been tread by faithful ones before you, and now you join that great lineage of those who follow Christ by following others who have followed Him well. This chain of discipleship strengthens us, guides us, and connects us more deeply to our Savior.

1 Corinthians 11:1 (NKJV) "Imitate me, just as I also imitate Christ."

In this chapter, we delve into the critical importance of **The Necessity of Discipleship** in the Christian walk. As believers, recognizing the role of following seasoned leaders is pivotal. This guidance is not merely about instruction; it is about shaping our spiritual journey, providing stability, and enriching our faith. This discipleship is how we learn, grow, and mature as followers of Christ.

Choosing whom to follow is not a trivial matter. It requires discernment and wisdom. When we talk about **Choosing**

Whom to Follow, we are referring to the importance of observing leaders who demonstrate consistent, long-term faith and integrity. Their walk with Christ offers us a pattern to emulate, a living example that informs and shapes our own pursuit of godliness.

In the realm of spiritual growth, **The Role of Spiritual Mentors** cannot be overstated. These individuals—leaders like Paul who said, "Imitate me, just as I also imitate Christ"—serve as tangible examples of living a life dedicated to following Jesus. Their lives provide a template that inspires and instructs us in practical and profound ways.

However, it's crucial to understand **Understanding the Boundaries** of this relationship. Spiritual mentors guide us to Christ; they do not replace Him. They hold a significant place in our lives but should never take the seat that belongs only to our Lord. This distinction helps maintain the purity of our devotion and ensures that Christ remains at the center of our worship and allegiance.

Discernment in Following is essential. It involves recognizing when a leader is deviating from the path that Christ laid out. This skill helps us decide when to draw close and when to distance ourselves from teachings or behaviors that do not align with biblical truth. Knowing when and how to follow is as crucial as knowing whom to follow.

The positive impact of following a godly leader is profound. **The Impact of Good Leadership** affects every aspect of our spiritual life, enhancing our understanding of Scripture, enriching our prayer life, and strengthening our community bonds. Good leaders not only teach us but also model for us how to live out the truths they preach.

One of the most humbling aspects of following a leader is **Learning from Mistakes**. Leaders are human; they err. Observing how they handle mistakes—how they seek forgiveness and correct their course—provides valuable lessons in humility and the importance of accountability. It also teaches us about the grace and restoration available through Christ.

In our admiration and respect for leaders, we must always guard against **Guarding Against Idolatry**. Our allegiance and worship belong to God alone. Respecting and honoring leaders should not cross into idolizing them, which can subtly shift our focus away from God.

For those who commit to a long-term discipleship relationship, **Long-Term Commitment to Follow** is key. This commitment should be nurtured through continuous prayer, engaging with Scripture, and participating in fellowship. It is a sustained effort that spans the duration of our Christian walk.

Lastly, **The Test of True Leadership** in our lives is whether those we follow lead us closer to Christ. They should not draw us to themselves but should constantly direct us to deepen our relationship with Jesus. This is the true mark of a leader worth following.

As we navigate the waters of discipleship, these principles guide us to not only choose wisely whom to follow but also to become leaders who are worth following, leaders who exemplify Christ in every aspect of life and ministry.

REFLECTIVE QUESTIONS

1. Who has been a significant spiritual mentor in your life, and how have they impacted your walk with Christ?
2. What qualities do you find most compelling in the leaders you choose to follow?
3. How do you maintain discernment and guard against

following leadership that does not adhere to Christ-like principles?

4. In what ways have you seen the impact of leadership influence your personal or spiritual development?

5. What steps can you take to ensure you are a positive and godly influence on those who may follow you?

ACTIONABLE STEPS

1. **Cultivate a deeper understanding** of the lives and teachings of those you follow. Study their lives, their teachings, and their legacy to ensure they align with biblical truth.

2. **Equip yourself with the knowledge and discernment** to identify when leaders deviate from biblical teachings. Regularly engage with Scripture and prayer to fortify your spiritual discernment.

3. **Engage actively in a community** that values biblical truth and godly leadership. This will provide a support system and a place to grow and share your journey with others.

JOURNALING **Prompt**

Reflect on your journey of following others in your faith. Consider the influences that have shaped your path, the lessons learned, and how you can apply these insights to become a leader who rightly guides others. Write about how this reflection might change your approach to who you follow and how you lead others.

CHAPTER 18
CASE IN POINT: WILLIAM BRANHAM

Let us take encouragement in the steadfastness required to faithfully follow the Lord, ensuring that we remain true to the teachings of Christ, and vigilant against the distractions that may lead us astray.

Hebrews 12:1-2 "Therefore we also, since we are surrounded by so great a cloud of witnesses, let us lay aside every weight, and the sin which so easily ensnares us, and let us run with endurance the race that is set before us, looking unto Jesus, the author and finisher of our faith, who for the joy that was set before Him endured the cross, despising the shame, and has sat down at the right hand of the throne of God."

In this chapter, we delve into the compelling journey of William Branham, a man whose life offers profound lessons for all who are called to carry a spiritual mantle. From his **Humble, Yet Supernatural Beginnings** in a Kentucky log cabin, marked by signs that predestined him for ministry, Branham's story begins as a narrative of divine election. This

109

startling introduction into his life's work reminds us of the unexpected ways God marks His chosen for great works, a calling that often transcends ordinary beginnings.

The powerful **Signs of Divine Calling** that followed Branham, including the voice directing him during his childhood and the ball of fire that visited his crib, were unmistakable markers of God's hand upon his life. These supernatural experiences are not merely historical anecdotes but are pivotal in understanding how God uniquely equips His servants. As followers of Christ, recognizing and responding to these divine interventions is crucial in stepping into the fullness of our callings.

As Branham's ministry progressed, it became evident that he was endowed with an extraordinary **Power of Anointed Ministry**. Miracles, signs, and wonders were regular occurrences in his meetings, affirming the power that follows obedience to God's call. This manifestation of divine power serves as an assurance to all believers that when God calls, He also empowers. It underscores the potential impact of a life fully yielded to God and challenges us to seek the same depth of relationship with Him.

However, Branham's life also serves as a sobering reminder of the **Dangers of Deviating from God's Call**. His later years, marked by doctrinal errors and a tragic departure from his initial ministry focus, illustrate the critical importance of remaining aligned with God's purposes. This shift not only affected his ministry but also had widespread implications for his followers. It is a stark warning that our spiritual integrity must be guarded with diligence and that deviation can lead to significant consequences.

The Importance of Corrective Mentorship becomes evident as we consider the lack of accountability in Branham's life during his deviation. This teaches us the value of having mentors who can offer correction and guidance, ensuring we remain on the path God has set for us. Mentorship is not just about encouragement but also about ensuring that we do not stray from the truth.

Branham's story also highlights the **Consequences of Isolation** in ministry. As he became increasingly isolated from corrective influences, his teachings began to reflect his personal interpretations rather than the truth of Scripture. This isolation can be a significant risk for anyone in ministry, as it often leads to a lack of accountability and an increase in susceptibility to error.

Through Branham's errors, we learn the crucial lesson of the **Impact of Misguided Teachings**. His incorrect doctrines had real, harmful effects on his followers, demonstrating how influential a leader can be—for better or for worse. This teaches us the necessity of doctrinal soundness and the responsibility of spiritual leaders to ensure their teachings align with biblical truth.

The Tragic End of a Misguided Ministry underscores the ultimate consequences of Branham's errors. His early death and the subsequent idolization by his followers serve as a cautionary tale of the potential end of a ministry not grounded in the truth. This tragic end prompts us to consider our own ministries and the legacy we wish to leave.

Finally, Branham's life story culminates in a call to **Redemption and Restoration**. Despite the missteps, the grace of God is always available to restore and redirect those willing to humble themselves and seek His face. This message of redemption is a beacon of hope for all who have strayed or fallen short in their spiritual walk.

By examining these key points in Branham's life, we are reminded of the complexity of spiritual leadership and the absolute necessity of grounding our lives and ministries in the truth of Scripture. As you reflect on this chapter, consider how you can apply these lessons to your own life, ensuring that you remain steadfast in your calling and effective in your ministry.

REFLECTIVE QUESTIONS

1. How can you ensure that your spiritual journey does not deviate from the path God has set for you?
2. What steps can you take to seek out and maintain effective mentorship in your spiritual life?
3. In what ways can you guard against the isolation that often accompanies positions of leadership?
4. How can you discern when teachings or doctrines deviate from scriptural truth?
5. What measures can you implement to safeguard the integrity and longevity of your ministry?

Actionable Steps

Cultivate a personal and communal prayer life that continually seeks discernment and guidance from the Holy Spirit.

Equip yourself with a thorough understanding of Scripture by engaging in regular, structured Bible study.

Engage in accountable relationships with other believers who can offer wisdom, correction, and encouragement.

JOURNALING Prompt

Reflect on a time when you felt particularly aligned with God's purpose for your life. What factors contributed to this alignment? How can you cultivate those factors today to ensure you remain on the path God has set for you?

CHAPTER 19

PASSING ON A MANTLE: NAVIGATING THE TRANSITION

Stand firm and be steadfast in your faith, knowing that God has prepared a mantle for you to carry. Embrace it with integrity and a willing heart.

"Be strong and of good courage; do not be afraid, nor be dismayed, for the Lord your God is with you wherever you go." - Joshua 1:9 NKJV

As we explore the profound concept of spiritual mantles, it is essential to recognize that **God Prepares Mantles for the Willing**. These mantles are not just symbols of spiritual authority; they are dynamic tools designed by God to fulfill His purposes on Earth. These are specially prepared for those who show a readiness and a heart aligned with God's divine intentions. Unfortunately, not all spiritual mantles find immediate successors. Sometimes, due to a lack of preparedness or willingness, **Mantles May Lie Dormant Due to Unpreparedness**. It is a sorrowful sight when such powerful tools of divine intention remain unused, waiting for someone to rise to the occasion.

The process of transitioning mantles from one generation to another is often fraught with challenges, primarily due to spiritual warfare. Our adversary does not sit idly by; thus, **The Enemy's Role in Blocking Transitions** is significant. The enemy employs various strategies to prevent these mantles from being passed smoothly, aiming to disrupt God's plans and delay His work on earth. Understanding this, we look to Scripture for wisdom and guidance. The Bible is rich with **Historical Examples Provide Lessons** on how to handle these transitions, offering both warnings and models to emulate.

A successful transition is crucial for the continuation of God's work. When a mantle is correctly passed on, it retains its divine purpose and power, a principle clearly illustrated in the transition from Elijah to Elisha. This shows the importance of ensuring a **Correct Succession**, which allows the seamless continuation of divine work without the loss of spiritual momentum. The consequences of failing in this task are dire, as seen when **Consequences of a Failed Succession** come into play, where the divine power and direction meant to influence generations can be significantly affected.

Personal integrity plays a non-negotiable role in the inheritance and successful carrying of a spiritual mantle. The story of Gehazi is a stern reminder that **The Role of Personal Integrity in Inheriting a Mantle** cannot be overlooked. Personal failings such as greed and deceit can disqualify one from stepping into a role divinely ordained for them. This leads to a critical understanding that **Mantles Require Active Participation**. Simply being in a lineage or position of potential succession does not guarantee the inheritance of a mantle. Active spiritual engagement, preparation, and alignment with God's commands are essential.

Despite the challenges, it is exciting to know that there is always the possibility for the **Revival of Dormant Mantles**. These mantles can be reactivated when the right person, prepared and willing, steps forward to claim them. This reactivation underscores the ever-present potential for revival and renewal within the kingdom of God. As such, **Preparing the Next Generation is Key** to ensure the continuity of God's work. As leaders and believers, we hold the responsibility to mentor, train, and prepare those who will follow after us, ensuring they are ready to pick up the mantles we leave behind.

In your journey of faith, remember that you are potentially the bearer of a divine mantle. Your readiness to embrace this call and carry it forward in power and truth can profoundly impact the kingdom of God, influencing generations to come.

REFLECTIVE QUESTIONS

1. How have you prepared yourself to receive and carry forward a spiritual mantle?
2. What steps can you take to ensure you do not block the transition of a mantle due to personal failings?
3. How can you actively engage in learning from historical examples provided in Scripture about mantle transitions?
4. What can be done to revive a dormant mantle within your community or spiritual circle?
5. How are you preparing the next generation to pick up the mantles you and others will leave behind?

ACTIONABLE STEPS

Cultivate an environment of readiness and willingness to receive a mantle by engaging in regular spiritual disciplines and seeking mentorship.

Equip yourself and others with knowledge and understanding of the nature of spiritual mantles through study and reflection on biblical examples.

Engage in activities that foster the development of personal integrity and spiritual maturity, essential for carrying a mantle effectively.

JOURNALING Prompt

Reflect on any dormant mantles within your own life or in your community. What are the steps that you can take to prepare yourself or help others to pick them up and carry them forward? Consider the barriers to picking up these mantles and how they might be overcome through prayer and action.

∼

CHAPTER 20
IT'S TIME!

Stand firm in the knowledge that every believer carries the mantle of Christ, our greatest treasure. This is not just a mantle; it is our identity in Him.

"But you are a chosen generation, a royal priesthood, a holy nation, His own special people, that you may proclaim the praises of Him who called you out of darkness into His marvelous light." - 1 Peter 2:9 NKJV

In this chapter, we delve into the critical understanding of **Mantles and Their Current Relevance**. Mantles, as we have learned, are not just artifacts of biblical times but are active and necessary in the current age. They are diverse and multifaceted, reflecting the varied ministries and callings that exist within the body of Christ today. The **Mantle of Christ**, as the ultimate inheritance of every believer, overlays and enhances any other spiritual mantle we might carry. It is this mantle that empowers us to live out our faith with authenticity and power.

Moreover, we explored how specific **Mantles Continue**

Under the New Covenant, each with distinct roles and purposes tailored to advance the Kingdom of God. These mantles are not just for individual glorification but are designed to equip the Church to fulfill its divine mandate on earth. As we recognize and embrace these diverse mantles, we see how they **Equip the Church for Diverse Ministries**, each contributing uniquely to the body's overall function and health.

The discussion around mantles is not complete without understanding the **Responsibility of Carrying a Mantle**. This responsibility is significant and should not be taken lightly. It requires a deep commitment to God's Word and a life lived in humble submission to His will. It's vital to recognize that **Mantles Require Holiness and Obedience**, as these are the prerequisites for maintaining their power and effectiveness.

As we look to the future, we see the importance of ensuring that **Mantles Are Passed to the Right Successors**. This passing is a divine act, orchestrated by God Himself, and is crucial for the continuation of His work on earth. The **Proper Succession of Mantles** is necessary to prevent the loss of spiritual authority and power that could otherwise move generations forward.

Lastly, we discussed the concept of **Corporate Mantles**, where God assigns mantles to entire congregations or groups, expanding our understanding of how God's power can manifest through collective entities in addition to individuals. This broadens our perspective and encourages us to seek deeper, more corporate engagements with the Spirit.

REFLECTIVE QUESTIONS

1. How do you perceive the mantle of Christ in your life, and how does it influence your daily actions?

2. In what ways can you prepare yourself to possibly receive or recognize a specific mantle within your community?

3. How does understanding the diversity of mantles change your view of the Church's role in the world?

4. What responsibilities do you believe come with carrying a spiritual mantle?

5. How can you contribute to ensuring the right succession of mantles within your own church community?

Actionable Steps

Cultivate a deeper understanding and appreciation of the mantle of Christ in your life through daily prayer and meditation on the Scriptures.

Equip yourself and others with knowledge about different mantles and their functions within the Church through study and teaching.

Engage in mentoring relationships within your church to help prepare the next generation for potential mantle succession.

Journaling Prompt

Reflect on the concept of the mantle of Christ and other specific mantles you might be aware of within your church community. How do these mantles manifest in everyday ministry, and what can you do to support or enhance the effectiveness of these divine empowerments in your life and in your community?

IT'S TIME!

Harrison House is a Spirit-filled, Word of Faith Christian publisher dedicated to spreading the message of faith, hope, and love through our wide range of inspiring publications. Committed to the messages that highlight the power of the Word and Spirit, we provide books, devotionals, and study guides that empower believers to live victorious, faith-filled lives.

Our resources are designed to help readers grow spiritually, strengthen their faith, and experience the transformative power of God's Word. Harrison House is passionate about equipping Christians with the tools they need to fulfill their divine purpose and impact the world for Christ.

www.ingramcontent.com/pod-product-compliance
Lightning Source LLC
Chambersburg PA
CBHW062113080426
42734CB00012B/2847